HELL LOST ANOTHER ONE

By

Frances Rodriguez

HELL LOST ANOTHER ONE

Copyright ©2023 by Frances Rodriguez
ISBN #979-8-9854594-7-0

TABLE OF CONTENTS

DEDICATION

I dedicate this book to my family, especially my cousin Esther for being my backbone. My dearest friends, The Holy One Church in San Antonio, Texas and Pastor Wendy Bustin for pushing me to my next. I love and honor you all! I declare a chain breaking anointing and supernatural blessings upon you all.

This book is in honor of my parents, Eddie, and Esther. My spiritual mother Lucy Sosa along with my family members who have entered their eternal resting.

CHAPTER 1
My life growing up

The enemy has been trying to take me out since before I was born. As a baby, I was overdue by two weeks. My mother was not able to give birth to me by my due date and had to be induced into labor - I was stuck. I remember my mother always describing my birth story by saying that the nurse had to literally get on top of her stomach to try and push me out. When I finally did come out, I was suffocating because my umbilical cord was wrapped around my neck.

So I believe that since that day, the enemy has been trying to stop me. It's like he didn't even want me to be born. At a young age, I continued to experience tough challenges that the enemy put in my path. When I was three years old, the enemy did not only take my innocence, but he also stole my identity. At the age of three years old, I was raped. I don't remember the actual rape, but I do remember the aftermath and the pain. I remember the police showing up to my house and that I was told to lie about what happened to me. I was told to say that I fell and hurt myself.

I can't recall if my parents were there when the incident happened, but I remember them being very afraid of not knowing what happened or even more so what was going to happen once the police showed up. I vaguely remember hearing my offender telling me to lie to my parents to say that I just fell and hit myself on the support bar of the swing set.

I distinctly remember the police officer coming and actually taking off my underwear and putting it in a baggy for evidence and seeing the blood on it. While I don't remember the actual incident, I remember that scene and the burning pain. The adults were scared that it happened and I was terrified. To this day, when I try to think about that day, I can still feel the burn. It not only traumatized me emotionally and mentally, but physically too.

My family was a very tight-knit family. My aunts all lived on the same block, so my cousins were more like my own brothers and sisters growing up. My grandmother's house was in the center of the block, so most of my cousins lived across the street and my other cousins lived a little further, about two houses down on the next block. All of the family lived close by so it seemed like we owned the block.

Grandma's house was the place where we would celebrate our holidays and everyone's birthdays. When my grandparents passed away, we eventually continued our family gatherings at the nearest aunt's house which was a little further down the block. That house then became the place for us to gather as a family. I grew up going to my aunt's to celebrate every Easter, Christmas, New Year's Eve and every other birthday.

Growing up, my parents didn't have much of a formal education. My father only went to school up until the fifth grade and my mother only went as far as third grade. They didn't know how to read or write. My mother could read a little, but my father couldn't; he knew how to do the math. My mother learned how to read mostly by reading the Bible.

When it came time for me to do my own homework in school, I really struggled because I didn't have anyone at home to help me or know what to do. At school, when we would be reading a story in class, when it came to be my turn to read aloud to the class, I would panic. The teacher would see me shaking my head in a panic as I thought to myself, "No, I can't read" and she would skip over me. I was held back in third grade because that's where I started to struggle a lot. Soon enough they put me in Special Education classes at school, mainly for reading.

I would just get nervous and embarrassed to read because I was so insecure of myself. During the reading classes, the teachers would come and pick me up to take me to the round building. The round building was where most of the special education classes were held. At first I was embarrassed to be in the special ed classes. But shortly after, I became more and more comfortable because it was more of a one on one learning experience and I didn't feel judged in class. I also wasn't asked to read aloud anymore in front of everyone, I would read to the teacher's assistant.

To top it off, in school I was always bullied; I've always been overweight. There was one little boy that would mock me as I walked past. With each step I took, he would act like the Earth was shaking and make the sounds like "BOOM!... BOOM!" I couldn't run after him to catch him, but what I would do is I would grab the closest boy next to me and tell him, "You better go and catch him, because if not, I'm going to beat you up!" They'd come back to me "Frances, I caught him!" and I'd finally get this little boy back. But in elementary school, I was always bullied until I made a boy cry. That was the end of me fighting boys, I really felt bad and embarrassed that I made him cry.

I was very tomboyish, and heaven forbid that anyone picked on any one of my girl friends in elementary. I always felt a need to protect them. When my friends would get bullied in school, they would come to me. "Frances, Frances, someone was picking on me!" I would say, "I will go find them." It was my desire to protect my friends that made me fight for them. Due to my constant standing up for my friends, I ended up being suspended for fighting.

Whenever I got in trouble at school, my father was there for me. He was the one who dropped me off at school and picked me up. Once I got to school, he would wait outside until I was inside. Every time I got into trouble at school, he was called to the office. He defended me at every opportunity when my school officials reprimanded me.

In order not to get in trouble with my mother, my father and I would go to McDonald's, Goodwill shopping, and spend the whole day together whenever I had to leave early from school for getting into a fight. Sometimes he'd just take me to the park and he would watch me play. He was always looking out for me. Sometimes he would even do the dishes for me when it was my turn, that's how I was spoiled by him. I had a really good relationship with him. It was only after his passing that I told my mom about how often I got sent home from school, as I didn't want either of us to get in trouble.

My mother and sister seemed to dislike me for a reason which I didn't understand. I was a daddy's girl. My father would leave for work, leaving my mother and sister alone with me. My Mom and sister were bullies, so the only person I could turn to for protection was my father. The bullying from my older sister and the mistreatment I received from my mother affected me throughout my childhood.

Some of my earliest memories of my childhood are of hiding under the bed when my dad came home drunk. On nights like these, my father would play Vicente Fernandez loudly, which served as a wakeup call for me to hide under the bed. I remember the music, yelling, and breaking of glass from dishes and TVs. Because he was so violent and unpredictable when drunk, I couldn't risk making any noise at all. I decided that if I just stayed where I was and did nothing, I'd be OK. Regardless of the occasion, my father always punished my sister the most; she was blamed for everything and beaten without justification. My father's treatment of my sister was just something I never understood.

Later in life I learned that my sister was not my father's biological daughter. My sister was conceived out of wedlock, then my father came into the picture when my mother was three or four months pregnant.

He gave her his last name, despite the fact that she was not his biological child. Nevertheless, we managed to work through it once it was brought to light and we were much older, but it took some time. My father never found out that we knew the truth. While there is no excuse for anyone being abused, it explained my father's anger towards her.

In comparison to my sister, I would get about a third of the fallout. My father's anger was always directed toward my sister. I was only beaten accidentally when I tried to protect her from him. Still, I could not stop him from hitting her. I felt helpless. Because I was unable to protect myself or my sister as a child, I am very protective of people now.

The way my father treated my sister had a lot to do with his own childhood. My father was rejected by his family as a child and as an adult. It must have been in his late 20's or so when my father discovered who his own father was. When he went to tell his dad, "I'm your son", his father just handed him some money and said, "Leave, don't ever come back." He always carried that pain of rejection with him. Eventually, my father, who at that time, may have been in his 60's, found him again. His father had no idea who he was; and my father pretended to be an ex-coworker of his.

He made up the lie so that he could talk to his half-brother and half-sister, then he called them and spoke with them. Each week, he would make his weekly call to his father on weekends. His father never knew it was him. Their relationship was never truly healed, but at least my father was able to get to know some of his siblings through these phone calls.

Towards the end of elementary school, my mother was involved in a major car accident where she almost lost her life. Before that accident, she did not live according to God's will. Consequently, at the early age of eight, I became her caretaker and my sister was forced to work when she was 13 years old. My sister was a mother's girl. She was always my mom's favorite. My sister had more freedom than I did. She went out more frequently with her friends. She would spend less time at home. That's why the full responsibility of my parents' care fell on me. The Fifth of the Ten Commandments reads: "Honor your father and your mother." This commandment carried a lot of significance to me, and I still honor and love them.

After my mother's accident, people gravitated towards my father because he became the most loving and joyous person. He was silly. He was funny. In some ways, he was almost like a loyal friend to me. He became someone I could always talk to, even though he was my parent. I believe he became more righteous when my mother stopped practicing witchcraft as a fortune teller due to her injuries from the accident.

Those dark moments were caused by the enemy coming to kill, steal, and destroy. That sin, the sinner, the bondage and strongholds of the enemy were then cast away from my parents.

During her healing, my mother turned completely to God and changed her life. Occasionally she would falter, but she remained devoted to Him. We all became more involved at our local Catholic church to support my mother. As a result of attending mass regularly, I developed my own desire to be kinder to people and serve God and I became more involved in our church community. At one point, I had expressed interest in starting the process to become a nun. I had started filling out all the paperwork because I was really interested in developing my faith through the Catholic church. My Priest and other church leaders wrote me letters of recommendation to become a nun in Chicago. However, my parents were so distraught over the thought of me moving out of state and stopped me from moving forward in the novitiate process and encouraged me to stay in school instead.

The most vivid memories I have of my mother are her prayers. No matter what, my mother always prayed for me. I believe that her prayers were answered, regardless of whether she agreed with my lifestyle or not. In my mind, I thought she only loved me because I was the only one who could take care of her. No one has ever done anything for me without some sort of intention behind it. However, she still taught me how to put on the armor of God, how to plead the blood of Jesus over myself and how to be a prayer warrior.

My mom was always this tough individual, very strong-willed. Even her siblings sometimes wouldn't want to be around her too much. Having been the oldest of eight siblings, my mother had to care for her younger siblings which influenced her personality. As the oldest, you are supposed to "know better" than your younger siblings. She was the built-in free babysitter that always had to set a good example.

The things you learn as a child stay with you forever. I remember getting into a bad situation and my mother was afraid I would go to jail. Even though she was already very ill, she got on her knees and prayed for me. That touched me deeply. Seeing your mother on her knees, begging and praying for you is enough to make you change your own life. Because of my mother's faith, I know how important a mother's love is.

When I pray for people now, I pray like I'm praying for the lives of my own children. I know how it felt to have a mother who loved me deeply enough to pray passionately for me. As a result, I would never want anyone to feel like they don't have a mother in this world. I pray for thousands of people a day. In doing so, my hope is that they will be able to feel God's love and grace at that moment, because it is so important. Knowing that someone is praying for you, loving you, and intentionally caring about you is so very powerful.

I am not perfect. I too make mistakes sometimes and fall short of the glory of God. In spite of that, I know there is power in prayer, which is what I learned from my mother through her faith and her prayers.

CHAPTER 2
The beginning of my strongholds

My teenage to young adult life was filled with good and bad times, but those are the moments that shaped me into the person I am today. My happiest and darkest moments often surrounded my church family. I loved going to church, it became my escape from all that was going on at home. I was a part of a youth group where we ministered and spread the word through speaking and performing skits to other teenagers. We traveled all over Texas to attend youth ministries and retreats. I was always the comedian in the group, and our skits brought joy to everyone who watched. It came so naturally to me. I loved making people laugh and sharing my love for Christ.

Although I grew up having a close family, my mother was very ill for most of my upbringing. She had been in a terrible car accident when I was only 8 years old. During the accident, the car flipped over and the rooftop came detached and scalped her. She had a traumatic injury to her skull and brain, but she was blessed to survive! They had to put a metal plate on her forehead in place of her skull, and she had over 150 stitches on her forehead and face.

After the accident, she couldn't really walk and had difficulty with her memory. I remember my father often reminding us, "Don't act afraid of your mom. Don't show her you're afraid, it'll hurt her feelings." At such a young age, I tried my best to be brave, but it was difficult to recognize my mother after the incident.

I can recall one particular evening, we were eating dinner. My mother was sitting across from me while we were at the table in the kitchen. At this time in her recovery, she still didn't have much control with moving her eyes, because of the intense brain trauma. I was eating my dinner but I was really afraid of her. I remember looking at her and her eyes just kind of popped out at me! I ran away from the table and screamed bloody murder as I ran to my room; I was so scared! I remember my father rushing after me to say, "You know, that really hurts your mom's feelings." Of course I was sorry, I didn't want to be afraid of my mother, but I was very young. Dealing with that type of rebuilding had many challenges.

Growing up after my mother's accident, there was not so much "motherly love" displayed in my childhood. It's not that she didn't want to give it, she physically couldn't. My mother couldn't even walk on her own or process the many moments she'd lived. Instead of getting to experience those 'Hallmark' moments of learning how to ride a bike, how to cook, and having help with our schoolwork with my mom by my side, my siblings and I had to see my mom relearning everything she once knew. She didn't just recover from one year to the next. It took plenty of years.

When I started going to the church, the first thing I noticed was I actually felt like a kid because I was in the youth group. I was finally able to have friends and be around more kids my age. I actually belonged somewhere.

In my church community, I met a lady who treated me like her own daughter. She quickly became a friend and mentor. I did not have a close relationship with my mother so she soon filled that void of a maternal figure. I honestly believed that this woman loved me as a mother loved a child. She would have the kids in the youth group all call her "mom" and her parents "grandma, grandpa." So it started to look and feel like I had a complete family.

This woman would spoil me and often give me money to buy anything I wanted. I remember one time she gave me $20! At the time, $20 was a lot of money to me, and I was not used to getting gifts, so it made me feel so special. She even gifted me a ring once, but I thought that she just liked buying me nice things. I did not understand the intentions of her actions or how my innocence as a child was being taken advantage of.

Each gift that I accepted seemed to give her more of a power over me. Being that I was so young and naive, I mistakenly viewed these gifts and actions as kindness, rather than an attempt to groom me. This woman was a well known church sister and chaperone on most events. No one - not even the adults - second guessed her intentions or her close relationships with the kids. We once had a getaway with the youth group. We had to sleep on sleeping bags. This one particular night, she signaled me to go sleep close by her. She wanted to have me near her.

Shortly after, she started to treat me like I was her possession. I was not allowed to be with my friends; she always wanted me physically close to her. As a result of what my parents viewed as an innocent friendly relationship, she quickly became a friend of family and was invited to all family events and gatherings too. Our romantic relationship started in high school and continued until early adulthood. As Christians, we're often taught about sacrifices that God requests that we make sacrifices throughout our faith journey.

I often interpreted my relationship with this woman as a necessary sacrifice to serve God, so I never shared what was truly going on with anyone. The devil was deceiving me. I was no more than 15 years old when our relationship started and she was more than twenty years older than me! In today's technologically advanced world, we have so many ways that older men and women can take advantage of our children. It is our job not to turn a blind eye even to the possibility of ill intentions.

This woman would lock me in her room whenever someone visited. The windows were nailed shut so there was only one way to enter and one way to leave. There was no escape. She made me believe that even if I mustered up the courage to share my abuse with someone that no one would believe me.

In my particular case, I believe that there must have been red flags but the people around us refused to acknowledge it, and in turn I was neglected and robbed of my identity as a young adult. The enemy comes to kill, steal and destroy. The first thing that the enemy will take is your identity, because he doesn't want you to know who you are. He doesn't want you to know that you are powerful, valuable and loved. After years of my relationship going unnoticed, I convinced myself that I was a lesbian and I accepted it as a part of my lifestyle and who I was.

My guilt, shame and self doubt made it easy for her to manipulate me in any way she wanted to. Everyone loved and respected her so I thought even with proof no one would want to believe that she would take advantage of me in that way. I thought that I had to sacrifice myself to protect other young girls from the sexual abuse I encountered.

In my mind, I thought my relationship was truly a sacrifice. As a Christian, you often hear that serving God is a sacrifice, and we have to make sacrifices for God. So I remember hearing that and thinking to myself, "Well, because I want to serve God, maybe this is my sacrifice that I'm supposed to give? This has to be my sacrifice." Being a teenager, I could only understand so much of that context of a 'sacrifice for God' that we are all called to do and expect. I loved God. I had always wanted to serve God, that calling has always been innate with me. So I figured that was the sacrifice I had to do in order to serve God. Because if I spoke out or if I said anything, then I was going to be removed from my friends or from continuing to serve other community members… from everything that I loved doing.

Now that I'm grown, I know the difference - there is a sacrifice in your walk with the Lord. You do sacrifice, but you sacrifice **you** in the flesh from doing the worldly things; but to a teenager, that relationship felt just as heavy as the sacrifices that my church leaders kept talking about.

When things turned for the worse in our relationship, at that point, I was just embarrassed. Because that's what the enemy wants to do. He wants to shame you. That was another situation to overcome as the enemy was just constantly shaming me and playing mind games with me. The strongholds - the tactics of the enemy are that he comes to kill, steal and destroy us.

I'm very familiar with the tactics of the enemy, I have to renew my mind daily and sometimes more than once a day to set myself straight. Especially on days when I'm reminded of the past. We have to be in the present and not be in the past, because the enemy will remind us of very real emotions and thoughts and use them against us as a distraction.

Growing up it felt that everything was swept under the rug and I was invisible. In my senior year of high school, my paternal grandmother suffered a stroke, so we brought her into our home and I took care of her. I had to play nurse during this time since she was on a feeding tube. I had a lot of responsibilities at a young age, so I kept a routine. The mornings were spent feeding my grandmother. During feeding time, the feeding tube became clogged quite often. Each time the feeding tube became clogged, I had to call the nurses and wait for them to arrive. It would be midafternoon by the time they arrived, resulting in me losing hours of my day. I missed a lot of school because of this, which meant that I missed out on many senior activities and classes.

It had such a detrimental effect on me that I was at risk of not graduating with my class. As a result of my numerous absences, I was told I would have to retake my senior year. My teacher suggested that I take my GED and then start college like everyone else. A GED certificate would serve as an alternative to a high school diploma. I thought, "How is that possible? How am I going to just get my GED? " Additional tasks would have to be completed before the exam, and I would have to wait for the exam to be offered. However, I wanted to avoid the embarrassment of staying another year. In the end, I opted for my GED rather than staying another year. I sacrificed again out of love.

In high school, I was in the ESL (English as a Second Language) class. At my school, our classes were mixed in; freshmen had classes with seniors depending on the subject. In elementary school, we were all in the same grade and we all took math at one time and reading and English together too. So when I got to high school, they didn't really know which English class to put me in and I got separated from my friends throughout the day. We had the same lunch period which was what mattered the most, but through that relationship in my life, no one really knew what I was going through. I just learned to smile through the pain no matter what this woman was telling me or how she was treating me.

As a teenager in high school, I was convinced that I was a lesbian, and pride kicked in. I really believed this is who I was, I was born this way. There was one boy that I thought was the cutest thing, but I always told myself that boys weren't for me. I didn't feel capable of being loved by a boy because my self esteem was so low and I struggled with being overweight.

I did have a crush on a friend of mine, but he was my friend, so it was a bit embarrassing. I remember I had a small rubber keychain with the school logo on it that we were given at the start of the school year. During class I had doodled, "Frances <3 ____" on it very faintly with a pencil. Months later, this friend was walking into class a few minutes late. He bent down by my desk and picked up something, "Frances, I think you dropped this" and handed me the keychain. I turned *beyond* red, I was so embarrassed! I snatched it out of his hand so fast, hoping he hadn't read it.

I hung out with a lot of my guy friends during Friday night football games and went out to eat as a group. But at the time, I didn't feel worthy of capable of being loved by a guy because in my mindset, I was a lesbian.

My mother and my sister disapproved of my sexual orientation, perhaps simply due to ignorance. Sadly, they made judgments about it. There was always the emphasis that it's a sin, how could I live like this? But the comments only fueled my pride. I always thought, "If God loves me, then why can't they love me?"

Years later I shared my story about this relationship I had with this woman who was my old church youth leader. At the time, my youth leader was the spiritual advisor leader at my new job. She had been waiting for her next group advising session to show up. but they never did. So an opportunity presented itself and I took it. It was not about exposing the woman who abused me but instead healing from my past trauma. Everyone praised her. Even my youth leader thought she was the nicest person and had no idea what our relationship was really like. Everyone assumed that whenever I was removed from the group, it was because I wanted to be but she controlled everything I did. It was one of the hardest things that I had to deal with. I felt like I had duct tape over my mouth for our entire relationship. I didn't have a voice.

Teenagers are supposed to have fun and be around friends but I never had the chance to just be a kid. I so badly wanted to ask my youth leader, "How could you have missed what was going on right in front of you?" but I didn't. I was trying to heal but I struggled to come to terms with what and how our relationship actually happened. Everyone admired her so even after I shared what happened to me I didn't think that my youth leader believed that I was telling the truth; but she looked at me with tears in her eyes and apologized repeatedly.

I felt so selfish because there I was trying to heal from my own trauma, but I was bringing pain to someone else. My former youth leader later shared my story with another spiritual brother who confirmed some of the details of my story. He was studying to be a priest and this same abuser would allow him to stay with her. One day he went into her room and saw the windows nailed shut just as I had experienced and had no clue why someone would do that. It always stuck with him because he could not figure out the reason until my youth leader shared my story with him. It broke their hearts to know they had missed the signs, but I did not want to dwell on the past.

My message to them was to forget about what happened and focus on where I am now and what God is doing for me. When my parents and sister found out, I was already in a new relationship. My sister wanted to take action against her but I disagreed. I worked so hard to move on from that part of my life and I was not interested in reliving the trauma and shame of my past. Even after I started dating, this ex would show up wherever I was. She would tell my partner that I was hers and I was always going to be in her life and no one could take me away from her. I felt so ashamed and I did not want the public exposure. It was a horrible situation but I still had an emotional bond to her.

CHAPTER 3
Trying to fill the void

In my adult life, I lived as a Christian while still indulging in all the pleasures of the world. It is essential for us to understand that God wants us to enjoy life, but there are certain guidelines for doing so. For a long time, I used alcohol and nightclubs to numb the pain of those early years. Despite my efforts to stay involved in the church community, my church struggled to accept me as a member.

I was convinced that I was a lesbian and I was born that way. I was convinced of that because of what the woman in my first 'relationship' had done to me. To me, identifying as a lesbian almost allowed me to exist in a comfort zone in my mind, because I didn't feel like I deserved to be loved by a man or anyone, and I was familiar with being loved by this woman. After a while, my personal dreams of actually having children of my own and starting a family of my own began to feel like it was taken away from me because of how intensely I claimed this sexual identification. I can't exactly explain the reasoning as to why I felt that way, but when the enemy has your thoughts in his control, it can be all-consuming. The enemy takes your identity in his mission to kill, steal and destroy.

When I found my thoughts to be distraught, I would try to find God. I would also attend church, but I would have to hide my true feelings. By that time, I was very familiar with hiding both who I thought I was and who I wanted to be. Everything in my life felt like either a secret or a lie to me, because I carried so much shame. The enemy comes to shame you. I was trying to live the life of the person that I was told to be and who I had acted out to be.

In the process, I was tough and strong. I had been carrying this burden alone and no one really knew the struggle that I faced within myself. I started to truly grow in Christ as I kept attending church. At church, I pretty much felt accepted. The congregation didn't really care who I was, I guess; I was just attending there, but I felt loved.

I would go to church on a regular basis, but I would also enjoy the club scene when I was just turning 21 years old. I would go out to the gay clubs as well. In this process of me returning to church regularly, I was still trying to be right with God because there was always that feeling of conviction in my mind, "This isn't really who you are." But…it was who I was told, no, *demanded* to be. When your mind is set, there's a very rare occasion that you're going to change it, your belief can become a fact to you.

Trying to be this Christian while still living in the world and its pleasures presented a lot of internal conflict for me. It's okay to enjoy life and have fun, but there is a difference between enjoying life as God allows you versus spending all your time incoherent while partying and drinking. God wants you to enjoy life, there's certain things we can do, but when you overdo it, it's not good. For me, I was always trying to numb the pain I felt. I didn't know of any other way to deal with it other than going to clubs and drinking.

There was once a vacancy for the president position in one of our Christian organizations. Since no other candidates were willing to assume the responsibility, I stepped up and volunteered to take on that role. To my surprise identifying as a lesbian excluded me from leadership roles in the church. In spite of no one else wanting the job, the church leaders held a meeting and it was unanimously decided that I was not a good fit for the position.

I couldn't express what I was feeling because no one in the room would have understood. While I looked and acted as if I was okay with their decision, their rejection broke me and caused me to drift further from God. I thought I would have been accepted and loved by my church community regardless of who I loved. Instead, I was judged and rejected at one of the lowest points in my life.

Everyone has a past and no one is without sin. No one should be excluded from the one community that should welcome you without judgment. It is only through love that people who are suffering from dark feelings can be healed.

As Christians, we have to be careful in how we deliver our messages to people. Maybe I was just too broken to begin with at the time, but it is often *how* we do things and how we communicate as the body of Christ that deters other people from feeling the welcoming hands and support of the church that they are supposed to feel. The leaders of the church decided that they would rather leave the position vacant than have someone of my sexual orientation fill it, but they could have explained it better. I was so hurt by that rejection that I left the church and went out into the world to live a life without God. We have to be careful, (yes, we all fall short of the glory) but it's the broken people that we need to show love and grace to, because someone once showed you that same grace.

The world started to feel like a friend at that moment and I thought that the world would embrace me more than the church ever could. During that time, I met my ex-partner, who I stayed with for 18 years. When we first met, we were both at a low point in our lives. She was a single mother of two young boys and an older daughter, who had just left an abusive relationship. I struggled with always wanting to help others even when it was not in my best interest. It was difficult for me to help someone without forming a relationship or an emotional attachment to them.

At the time when we met, I was going out to clubs and doing my own thing. We exchanged numbers when we were coworkers at the group home, for months we would carry on friendly conversations when passing by each other at work. One night I noticed she hadn't brought anything to eat for lunch and she explained that she didn't get a chance to eat anything because she was trying to put her boys to sleep before she had to leave for work. I offered, "I can pick you up something to eat if you'd like!" because I'm the type of person that when someone tells me they're hungry, I'm going to feed them and care for them.

I took a trip to McDonalds to get her some food and I learned that she had two young boys, one was 2 years old, and the other was 3, and she also had a 16 year-old daughter. We got to know each other better by going on lunch dates to grab food in between shifts and dealing with situations at thegroup home. She worked in the night shift from 11pm - 7 am on the outskirts of the group homes on the campus that housed the group homes. Each home or "cottage" as we called them had its own phone number for the building. Earlier on in our friendship, there were a few incidents of a creepy guy lurking around that campus. She would call or text me while she was at work worried about this random man and what he was doing.

He would call each of the cottages at all hours of the night and go around knocking on the windows shouting at the attendants, "I'm watching you. I see what you're doing!" Many coworkers had filed police reports and this had been going on for quite some time but they weren't able to catch him. All of the night staff was pretty shook up, because most of the team that worked at night were women. One evening, she texted me freaking out, "Frances, he's here! He's outside, he just called my cottage and saw me. He read what was on my shirt. He's outside my cottage!" I was also working that night and I let the other staff members know that this man was on campus.

When this man would show up, there was nothing these women could do except to call the police and hope they got on site in time to catch this man in the act. They couldn't leave the cottage unattended in the middle of the night, so we made a plan to try and catch this man the next time he stepped foot on the campus. I offered to go outside and confront this man while the other women would come outside the front door to protect the doors so he couldn't sneak in and so that somebody was watching my back too.

After my partner alerted us he was there that night, I snuck outside to the back door and I saw him and asked, "What are you doing?"

"I'm the maintenance man," he replied. "I came to check on the pool."

"I don't believe that's what you're doing here," I yelled. "You need to stop coming here and calling and scarring these women!"

Of course he acted like he didn't know what I was talking about, but I was able to confront him and provide more details about him to the police so they could take care of the rest after we caught him.

My coworker and I began interacting more and more especially after this series of incidents because she would call me when she was afraid and I was able to help protect my fellow coworkers by helping to handle the situation. As time went by, we became friendlier and friendlier. In all reality, I didn't see her in any other way outside of a friend, because at the time, I was still convinced that I was in a committed relationship with the chaperone from my youth group.

Out of nowhere, during a shift change at work, my coworker friend said to me, "If you're going to kiss me, just kiss me." At this point, I was wild and wasn't looking for any kind of relationship. I was still emotionally attached to my first relationship, but I ended up kissing her. In my mind, I wasn't thinking she would have any romantic interest in me because she was straight.

She had a rough upbringing and not as many positive experiences with people. Her mother had abandoned her at a young age. In her teenage years she didn't have anything, and she told me stories about having to sleep and eat out of the dumpsters in the city with her brother or about how she went to steal shoes from a grocery store that sold them, and she was so nervous that she walked out with two different sized shoes. One was two sizes too big and the other barely fit.

When I met her, she was on the run from an abusive relationship from the boys' father. He would put fear in her by threatening to hurt her or kill her. She was in a group home and working to make ends meet. She would call me every night and I would listen to her talk about her day and her situation, and lend a listening ear. She never really had anyone to care for her, and in just being myself, I had no intentions of starting a romantic relationship, but I did intentionally show her love, care, and protection.

As a friend, I decided to embrace that responsibility to fill the void in her life. Her boys were so innocent and pure at only two and three years old. I loved them unconditionally as if they were my own. I was happy to assume the maternal responsibility and role in their lives. It was always my dream to have two boys, but when I started living this lifestyle, I didn't know how I would be able to have children, so I gave up that dream. This relationship allowed me to form a bond with the children who would love me as much as I loved them. I became the breadwinner for her family and the working parent in our new found relationship.

The boys were both wonderful. The oldest was naturally more independent and introverted and the youngest was very affectionate and extroverted. My partner and I loved the boys so much, and so did my parents. It was wonderful watching them grow up from such a young age to the young men they are now.

The youngest boy was really attached to my father and mother. He knew that my mother always loved going to the salon and getting her hair and nails done weekly. When she was in better health, but still needed assistance in getting around, the youngest would often take her to the salon and they would have their own little moments together.

They were so close, that when he brought up the idea of getting a tattoo, although he was only 16 or 17 years old, my mother told him he would have to drive, but that she would sign the parental consent form if he wanted a tattoo. His mother didn't mind the thought, but I told her, "Mom there's no way you're taking him to get a tattoo!" She would always try and spoil him in her own ways. They had so many wonderful memories together.

The youngest would show his emotions more outwardly than the oldest, but there were times when the oldest would bond with my parents and share his experiences with them. He had just started high school when he decided that he wanted to start working. He ended up getting a job at a local BBQ restaurant and I remember when he shared the news, "I got the job" with us over dinner, my mother just gave him a little hug and told him, "I'm so proud of you. Soon you'll be able to start saving money and taking care of what you've worked for." She would often give him grandmotherly advice like that once he was a teenager.

Although my parents didn't approve of the relationship I had with my partner, they loved the boys like we loved the boys. Eventually, after so many years they pretty much accepted our relationship. We were together for a very long time and she and the two boys became a part of the family.

Going grocery shopping is one of the things that my ex, the boys and I would spend a lot of time doing together. When the boys got a lot older, of course, then it was just us two doing the shopping but I was still buying for a whole full household.

We had our own place together but when my parents' health started to deteriorate we moved in with them. I went to school and worked two jobs to provide for my family and while I was away my partner helped take care of my parents. She only worked 2 full time jobs for a couple of the years that we were together. Most of the time she took on odds and ends jobs after her time at the group home where we met.

One of the first jobs she had for about two years when the boys were younger. As the boys grew older she worked various part time jobs to be able to spend more time with them and make sure they were taken to and from school and to take care of the house. We moved in with my parents when the boys entered their elementary years. She ran errands for my parents, prepared meals, and cleaned the house while I was at work. The condition of my dad's health continued to deteriorate, and he was diagnosed with cancer.

My father was my world. I did not want him to face his illness alone so I never left his side. It was important to me that he felt loved and supported. I would come home from work after working a 12 hour shift and take a two-hour nap before getting up to take my father to chemotherapy three times a week. I accompanied him to every doctor and chemotherapy visit.

Eventually caretaking and working full time became too much to manage, so I left my job at the hospital and became a full time provider for my parents. I eventually got a job working overnight at a women's shelter to earn extra income. In spite of not bringing in much money, I was able to fully care for and spend quality time with my parents with the help of my partner.

Not long after my father's diagnosis, she took an assignment working with a supplier for a motor vehicle company in a different state, and that was odd to me, but it was income! At the time, I was the home provider for my parents and the boys. I would bring home some extra cash from working at the shelter. My partner worked 3-11pm but she would often work overtime or have to stay overnight when she worked out of state.

CHAPTER 4
The crushing of my heart

My father continued to do chemotherapy and radiation for five years until he got to a point where he was tired of treatments and decided to go into hospice care. I was sad to watch him go but I held his hand until he transitioned. My partner's youngest boy was very close, almost attached, to my father.

After my father's passing, the youngest boy went out into the middle of the street crying and blocking the road because he didn't want anyone coming to pick up his grandpa and take him away. It was so hard for me after my father passed too. I missed him so much. I wore black every day for a little over a year to mourn his death. It was a tradition back then in the Hispanic culture. It was my way of showing the world that I had lost one of the biggest part of my world. I did not leave the house, watch television or listen to the radio for about three months after he passed.

My mother's health also started to be of concern after his death. We would have to call the ambulance almost every day because she was constantly complaining of chest pains. We assumed it was because of issues with her pacemaker, but on one of our doctor visits a nurse told us that she was suffering from a broken heart. At the time I was struggling with my own anxiety and depression but I kept pushing myself for her. She became bedridden and could not manage to do everyday tasks on her own. Mentally, she went back to being a little girl who needed to be taken care of.

It wasn't until further along in my relationship that I noticed my partner had become a little possessive of me. In relationships, it can be easy to turn a blind eye to manipulation at the beginning. She would offer to pick me up and drop me off at the hospital which started out being really convenient.

I have always just loved other people, and with my relationship with her, obviously my love was intended to be a friendship, not an assignment. I saw my partner when she was a struggling single mother and she would have to leave her boys with her oldest daughter and go days without food for her family.

But her demeanor for doing simple favors like this had changed over time... She would drop me off, and pick me up and but it felt like she was offering to do so in a controlling manner, almost like she was my parent. There were times where I would be so embarrassed waiting outside, seeing my co-workers coming outside and I would still be sitting waiting for a ride for 30-45 minutes because my partner overslept. I would even have to call my father many times when he was still in good health and ask him to check on her at the house if she was awake or if she remembered when I needed to be picked up. After working a long 12 hour shift, I just felt so drained and tired of waiting to go home to start my next job as a caretaker. That gesture that started out as a convenience seemed to become a great inconvenience later on.

I started noticing other elements in our relationship had shifted around this time too. I am not the type of person to be suspicious or constantly checking another person's phone. But my partner would leave for work early and often come home late. I was the caretaker for my parents and the boys full time so I started to notice a pattern. I would hear her talking on the phone a lot to another woman, who I assumed was a friend.

One particular weekend we were at her sister's house for a party and she gave me her phone to hold while we were taking family photos.

I could see that this female friend she always spoke to had called and left a voicemail. So I pressed play in front of everyone, "Hey girl! Oh my God I missed you! My sister told me you had come to surprise me and you were waiting here for me." At that time, phones didn't have passwords or anything. I was in shock. My partner turned bright red. Her brother and sister in law were sitting there with their mouths hanging open. Our relationship wasn't the same after that day.

I was heartbroken and hurt. It felt like my heart had been pierced with a knife. I was so embarrassed and shocked because I had been taking care of the boys to support her when she was working her job out of town. I clearly began to see that the last 6 months of tension in our relationship was a result of a lack of trust that had been developing and the added dissonance with her working out of town wasn't helping us mend any of our issues. The infidelity explained our change in behavior and allowed for more toxic and manipulative interactions between us.

The drive back to our house that night was silent. I didn't want to argue in front of the boys. A few of her family members messaged me asking if I was okay and saying that I didn't deserve to have to go through this. She never admitted to cheating, and made many excuses for it.

We decided to work through this difficult time and stay together because she and the boys didn't have anywhere to go, our home was her only home. When we first developed a relationship, it was because I cared for her and truly cared for the boys and I wanted them to have the best life possible. My partner and I fell in and out of love over time, but we didn't start our relationship because one of us was swept off our feet, head over heels in love. Shortly after I found out about the other woman, she stopped working the job out of state.

At this time, my mother became bedridden and could not manage to do everyday tasks on her own. Mentally, she went back to being a little girl who needed to be taken care of and she had a hospital bed at the house. On her bad days, I would be awake through the night to help her. I would sleep very little because she would always try to get up from her bed in the middle of the night. Her hospital bed had railings around it, and an alarm that would go off every time she tried to get up.

One particular morning, around 3:00 am, I heard her alarm go off and I went to go check on her. I still have no idea how my mother was able to get her legs stuck in between the thin metal bed rails as she tried to get up. My mom wasn't a thin person. So I asked, "Mom, how did you do this?" and she explained, "I have no idea, I just wanted to get up and go to the restroom!" Many times I would doze off to sleep just for a minute before putting her bed rails up for the night and she would be stuck or sometimes fall in the middle of the night.

She once began to cry because she was afraid that her father would hurt her. I heard her scream, "He's coming and he's getting a gun." She was reliving a traumatic experience from her past that I had no knowledge of. At that moment, she was crying and panicking, and all I could do was comfort her and let her know that she was safe. It was then that I understood her love for me. I had no idea what she had gone through in her childhood.

It is difficult for someone to give you something that they never had, so at that moment it all made sense to me. She carried all that pain for 74 years. The fact that she re-lived that moment with her father on her deathbed shows just how much that moment impacted her life. Back then, everything was swept under the rug and remained hidden your entire life. Despite what someone did to you, nothing would be said or done about it. She had always been this hard person with a very strong personality.

As the oldest of eight children, she had always taken care of everyone else, so she was not used to anyone taking care of her. I would take her to the restroom, move her in and out of her wheelchair, and bathe her. She loved getting her hair and nails done so I learned how to do it for her. I was not very good at it but I still tried my best to make her feel classy and beautiful even though we spent most days at home. Over time my mother's health continued to worsen until she passed.

After losing my mother my whole world changed. I lost my reason to live. I spent my whole life honoring my mother and father and now that they were both gone, I was so lost. I started experiencing excruciating pain all over my body so I used my mother's wheelchair and cane that she left behind. At this point I was diagnosed with gout, fibromyalgia, depression, anxiety and bipolar psychosis. My illness was treated with more than 22 medications. I was spiritually, mentally and physically broken.

My cousin made me a Godmother to her two children and they gave me hope in my dark moments. There were times that I was so depressed that I did not want to leave my bed but I would find the strength to stand up because I knew my god daughter would be visiting me soon. Years later I was blessed with my sweet godson.

My only glimpse of life was my godchildren. Despite my own pain I tried to support and love them unconditionally. I treated them like they were my own and spoiled them in any way that I could. God used them in my life to give me strength and courage to keep living. I believe they are the reason why I am still here today. Food and Netflix became my coping mechanism to deal with all the pain that I was feeling. As a result I weighed about 385 pounds and I couldn't do much for myself.

It got to a point where I could not even manage to put on my own bra. I did not have any income, so I could not even afford to buy one of the bras with the clips on the front. My partner would use that to remind me that I could not live without her. I could not manage to do basic everyday tasks on my own. She constantly spoke negatively about my life and belittled me in any way that she could. The enemy wants to control you and have power over you. I was so broken that I believed everything that she said.

My health was deteriorating and my self-esteem was low. Her sons were one of the most rewarding parts of our relationships. In the beginning despite working all day, I continued to make every effort to stay as involved as possible in the boys' lives. I planned fun family outings and got them involved in all the activities; they enjoyed karate and football. Whenever my schedule allowed, I always made every effort to be at their practices and games.

As boys, they loved their name brand shoes, so when I was making good money at the hospital, I always tried to save a little extra or look for sales of their favorite Jordans. The most important thing to me was to make them happy. I loved and supported them in any way I could, but I did not really know how to be a parent. It was a generational struggle. My parents did not have a perfect upbringing so it influenced how they were as parents. I wanted to give the boys everything that I never had. They truly were good boys and I wanted to give them the best life possible.

When my partner and I met, we were both broken and hurt by our past. As a consequence, she reflected her pain and insecurity in the way she treated me. I mistook her control for kindness and love.

Other than controlling my ride to and from work, my partner also began to control me in small ways, from the way I did my hair to who I spoke to. I am an outgoing person and I often enjoyed talking with new people but she was always jealous, despite the fact that it was innocent. This led to constant arguments between us but we were willing to work on our relationship and find God together. As a same-sex couple we struggled to find a church where we belonged.

We were once invited to church by my sister and as soon as we walked in, the pastor started pointing his finger at us. The entire service was spent publicly disapproving of our lifestyle and being told we would be going to hell. We were so embarrassed. All we wanted was a judgment free community to serve God and hear His word. I understood their issues with my relationship but that was not the way to do it. I felt so bad because I invited my partner to come with me and unknowingly exposed her to that negativity. I left with my head hanging in shame, feeling worse than how I felt walking in. Eventually we moved on and talked ourselves out of it. We knew that we would eventually find a church community that embraced us.

The next church we attended was her sister's. Although the service began well, when the pastor went to the altar we once again became the focus of the sermon. We were described as sinful women and publicly shamed for our sexual orientation. It was hard to deal with the constant rejection from the church community. Imagine trying to find a way closer to God and experiencing constant shame from those who should represent Christ and his characteristics - caring, loving, kind and accepting. Every time there was a glimmer of hope it was torn down again but we still continued to try to build a strong relationship with God.

We had our own bible studies at home and reminded ourselves that God loves us all. It didn't matter what the people around us said or how many times the pastor tried to convince us otherwise we knew God loved us. Eventually we found a church specifically for the lesbian, gay, bisexual, transgender, and questioning, LGBTQ, community. It was filled with the most loving and accepting people. Our lifestyles were similar, so we understood the struggles we faced because of it, so we accepted each other and helped to fill the void. It was an opportunity for me to worship God and learn about His word without judgment.

I often felt uncomfortable in other churches because they disapproved of my lifestyle. Since I had this spirit of offense always with me, even if someone was having a bad day on their own, I would assume the expression on their faces was one of disapproval of me. In my new church, however, you were free to be yourself without worrying about being judged. We formed a family and helped each other in any way we could. For fun, we went bowling, watched movies, to the zoo and played board games - without judgment. I felt truly included in every single moment with this church and they became like family to me.

My spiritual mother loved me unconditionally, with no other intention than to better my life so that I could become the person I am today. It was she who taught me to love myself and embrace my brokenness. I was reminded to not care about what people think or say about me because I am worthy of God's love. In Hispanic culture, we tend to hide a lot of things from others due to our concern of their perception of us.

She taught me that we have one audience; God. When God speaks to me, He is not talking to anyone else. I learned that my conversation with God is not a conference call, but an intimate conversation with Him and myself. Through her, I strengthened my faith and was inspired to be fearless and to live a bold life. My faith taught me that I could handle anything since Christ lives within me. She gave me the wake-up call I needed to take control over my life again.

After I lost my parents, I felt like I was living in my own hell. The commandment, "Honor thy mother and father," was a staple of my purpose. When my parents passed I didn't really know what else to do with my time or how I could honor my mother and father. In that early time of grief, I had lost my sense of purpose for my life, and soon after, I started to become physically sick.

We kept many of my parents' things in the house, particularly my mother's walker and wheelchair. Because of my size, I would make use of the walker and wheelchair throughout the day. What seemed like a convenience quickly became a curse. In a few months time, I became dependent on the walker to get around the house, and I began asking my partner, "Can you wheel me to the restroom?"

My depression and anxiety had set in badly alongside the grief. I was diagnosed with fibromyalgia, gout, and arthritis because of my weight, and of course; anxiety and depression. I was taking 22 medications a day - sometimes more. Occasionally I was high on so many pills that I would hallucinate. Sometimes I would feel so guilty that I was still alive.

When my mother's health was in decline, she was receiving hospice care full-time. To offset the depressing energy of my mother's situation, I often had time to babysit my godchildren. They brought so much joy to my life in those days. They were my inspiration to want to wake up because at the time I was dealing so much with my mom's health. Once the kids would leave, and the hospice caretaker would leave, I would keep busy with attending to my mother's remaining needs. Some nights she would keep me busy, and I'd end the day taking a long shower, relaxing and going off to sleep before my head even hit the pillow. Other times, I'd have sleepless nights if my mom was having a bad day or continuing to feel ill during the night. By taking care of both my godchildren and my mother, I would wear myself out.

I remember the emptiness I would feel after my godchildren would return home for the day when I was caring for my mother. After they left, I felt like I was in hell again. I experienced that same hell every day after my parents died. I had been heavy set my whole life, but in this grieving period I would eat ice cream, drink soda and partake in all those unhealthy foods. I tried filling the void with comfort foods, resulting in me gaining unhealthy weight.

I was tired and did not want to live anymore. I was being controlled in my relationship and I felt like I did not have anything left. My partner's boys were getting older and doing their own thing. At the end of the day, I was not their mother, they had their mother.

I did not have anyone, so I felt all alone. I started to believe that anything was better than the hell that I was going through. To get around the house, I would need to use a walker. Sometimes, I couldn't even get out of bed because of the physical pain that I was in. When you go to the doctor and you tell them you're in pain, they usually give you pain medication. It would help numb the pain, but it would never eliminate it, because I was experiencing the physical effects of so much emotional pain. So I added those to my 22 medications.

Some days I would just lay in bed, waiting to die. I felt tortured by the negative thoughts in my head. I thought I was going to hell and even that would have been better than what I was going through. I had spent all my life taking care of other people and doing kind things for them and I was never taught how to truly care for myself.

Now I rebuke it, but at that point my world was empty and with all the medications I was on I could barely function. I felt numb. One day, I grabbed a gun and wanted to end it all…

CHAPTER 5
In the pit of my own hell

My partner came into the room and seeing the fear in her eyes distracted me from my own pain at that moment. She saw that blank look in my eyes and knew I was gone. She begged me to put the gun down. She then ran to the living room and started screaming and crying. I felt horrible.

Her loud outcry snapped me out of it and caused me to put the gun down. I joined her in the living room. She just looked at me with tears in her eyes and hugged me. I don't think she understood all the pain I was feeling until that moment. Control was becoming such a daily part of our lives; I don't think she saw it for what it was.

She had her flaws but I put her through hell too. It was a toxic relationship but I wasn't perfect either and I played a part in the issues in our relationship. When we met, she was broken and I was broken too. Just because we come into contact with someone and we're able to help, please know that not everyone is your assignment or your responsibility to fix.

My breaking point in our relationship was when my partner prevented me from taking my aunt to the hospital. I have always been the go-to person in my family; I am ready to help in any way that I can. My aunt had recently become very sick so she visited the hospital frequently. She lived across the street, so I'd usually check in on her once she got home from her hospital visits.

One particular day, my aunt had just gotten back from the hospital. I spoke with her that day and she still wasn't feeling well, so I wanted to take her back to the hospital immediately. My partner wasn't able to help me in assisting my aunt. At the time, I had difficulty getting up and around even with a walker by myself. Later that morning, I called a family member of mine asking if they had heard from my aunt. They mentioned she was starting to feel better, so I didn't worry about her.

A couple of hours later, my cousin and her coworker stopped at her house to check in on her and she saw her lying lifeless on the floor. Her coworker ran across the street to come get me from my house and we all rushed back over to her house. While they called 911, I did chest compressions to try to bring her back but my efforts were unsuccessful. When the EMS team came we were asked to leave the room while they worked.

I remember kneeling on the porch steps praying and begging God to bring her back to life. I prayed like I never have before. Like I saw my mother do for me. I was not ready to lose her too. I begged and pleaded with God to bring her back to us. I knew I was not living the most righteous life; I was living in a same sex relationship while also living in bondage of the labels that other people gave me for my life. I thought that I could negotiate with God - that if he saved her then I would change my life. The EMS team tried until there was nothing else they could do to revive her. I was beyond heartbroken. I felt like I was being rejected by God, but instead of drifting away from his word I submitted myself to Him.

I thought that my prayer was not answered because I was not living my life according to his word so I took ownership of my wrongdoings. My lifestyle was never really wrong in my eyes because God loves us all so I did not believe that who I chose to love, whether man or woman, would influence his love for me.

I read the Bible and went to church to try to get closer to him regardless of the constant rejection and judgment from various church communities. To have begged and pleaded with him to breathe life into my aunt and it not happening was the biggest blow in my life. I was the core of the family. My family depended on me so at that moment I felt like I had let them down. I started self-medicating on top of the 22 prescribed pills that I already had. I was hoping for some relief from the pain I was feeling, but my pain was not physical so nothing worked.

I was tired and done being controlled by my partner. Her thoughts were always from a place of jealousy, but I entered into her life in the role of a provider - so I can understand not wanting the fear of losing that provider for her family. Somebody just doesn't become controlling overnight. Perhaps spending time with other LGBTQ+ church families made me pay more attention to behaviors in my relationship that otherwise I would have overlooked.

As I mentioned before, my ex-partner would control me in ways of not allowing me to fellowship with other people. It felt like she didn't want me to spend time with anyone else. If we were out and about, and someone was even friendly to me, it would be an issue to argue over once we got home that I had a polite interaction with another person. To me, these would be friendly conversations, but in her eyes, it was often mistaken as a flirtatious interaction. The other elements of control would go as far to forbid me from dying my hair. I also couldn't go out of my way to help my family sometimes because she would say things like, "they have other family members, they're not your responsibility."

Shortly after the situation with my aunt, I confronted my partner and told her that I was leaving and there was nothing that she could say or do to change my mind. The guilt of not being able to help my aunt or at least tricking my gut into thinking that my aunt would be okay ate away at my core. It was a life or death situation for my aunt, and I had put myself in a place to depend on someone else to help me be there for her.

When I prayed my heart out asking God to give her life and it didn't happen, I had a revelation that I had been the one to not stand up for myself and what I felt in my heart that I needed to do for my aunt in that situation. I had given up control over both my body and my mind, by putting unhealthy things into them. Now I'll never know the answer to the question: if I had been able to help her myself, would my aunt still be around?

The bottom line for most things in my life at that time was that I *allowed* them to happen. My rejected prayer from God made me feel like I was rejected by God. That made me snap out of it! Out of that rejection, arose a warrior, a *true* fighter within me. It was almost like a flame ignited and since then, no one - no devil, no demon has taken it from me. It made me somehow realize that what the enemy meant for evil, by controlling my mind and my body in whatever way he could, God turned it around. God woke me up!

Now when I am in prayer, there is a shift, and I know that I come to prayer with a complete understanding of the full authority of God. It has been because of that prayer that didn't come to pass when I was praying for my aunt that I know with my heart that God is in control and he has the final say. Now when I pray, there's something different in my prayer. That fighting spirit - maybe it was the holy spirit - that drove me to say, "I'm done. I'm out."

My partner replied to me telling her that I was leaving by using her manipulative tactics to try to convince me that I couldn't live without her. She told me that no one could have me if she couldn't. I did not care what she had to say. I called my sister and told her to come get me from the house. We were still living in my parents' house but I did not care. I told her that she could take over the mortgage and it would now be her responsibility.

That night she sat on the loveseat in our room silently watching me with tears in her eyes as I packed. I remember waking up at 3am to use the restroom and seeing her in the same position. I was still unbothered by her reaction. Nothing could change my mind at that point. I was done with our relationship and I had to leave our home. When I woke up in the morning my partner walked into the room and said to me "I tried to kill you last night while you were sleeping". I replied, "You did?". She continued," Yes, I put the gun to your head but the gun would not go off". I was so angry, not because she wanted to kill me but because she didn't succeed in pulling the trigger.

I remember repeatedly asking her why she didn't do it. She replied "The trigger didn't go off!" I was so mad at her for not doing it, because if she had succeeded in pulling the trigger all this pain that I was feeling would have finally ended. I felt a sense of rejection. God did not want me and the devil did not want me. I had no escape.

Even though I was disappointed that she did not succeed with her intentions, her actions made my decision to leave much easier. She decided that she did not want my parents' house, but my sister was already on her way from Dallas so I stayed with my sister at a hotel for three days while my partner packed.

When I went home, the house was completely empty - even the toilet paper was gone. She took everything except for one of the appliances, which she later came back for. My sister tried her best to encourage me. She bought me a sofa set but she still didn't feel comfortable leaving me like that so she convinced me to go to Dallas with her.

Everything I had worked so hard for was gone so I felt so defeated. I have always been so independent, so having to move from a house to now sharing a room with my youngest niece as a grown woman was hard. But there was no more fight left in me, so I packed all that I had left and decided to move in with my sister.

It was unconditional love and an accepting community from that LGBTQ+ friendly church that helped me to grow and heal from my past. As I got more in touch with my spirituality and the word of God it opened my eyes to how controlling my partner was. I started to notice how the enemy was trying to consume my mind.

It was not an easy decision to make, but I had nothing left in me to keep fighting…

CHAPTER 6
The power of fasting

After experiencing everything, I realized that I needed a fresh start so I moved to a new city with my sister. In my parents' house I shared so many good and bad memories, but most recently all my memories of that house were sad ones. I needed a new beginning to heal from my trauma. It killed me to leave behind my godchildren during the move. That was the worst, they had been such a pillar in my life. The separation was tremendous, I can't even describe the heartbreak I felt. I was around them for at least 12 hours a day.

They boys were a huge part of my life. I had to leave them, but I still could cry now recalling how painful it felt to leave them. But this was my chance to become the person I always wanted to be without being haunted by my past. When I moved, I made every effort to fully integrate myself into my new environment. I went from leading and providing for a whole household to now sharing a room with my youngest niece.

My sister had such amazing things to say about her relationship with her church that I was ready to become a part of her community. They were extremely supportive and played an integral part in healing at the lowest point in my life. It was so hard for me to change my entire lifestyle to remove my destructive and self-harming traits to heal my mind.

Through the church I met my spiritual mother Lucy who loved me unconditionally, with no other intention other than to better my life so that I could become the person I am today. It was she who continued to teach me that I was worthy to be loved by God. My faith taught me that I could handle anything since Christ lives within me. She was my life line when I wanted to give up. She would drive an hour to come pick me up and distract me from the pain. She gave me the wake-up call I needed to take control over my life.

I moved to Dallas, Texas on December 22nd of that year so it was right before the new year. That's when my whole life changed. Usually my New Years plans involved getting drunk and partying all night, but that year I started my new year with a midnight church service. I had never rung in the New Year at church so it was different.

It was so refreshing to start the new year worshiping God and learning about His word. I felt like I was setting the tone for the rest of my year by starting the right way. I felt alive for the first time. It was both frightening and thrilling at the same time. I was so numb from taking so many medications that I did not remember the last time I really experienced any positive emotions.

Since I didn't have a doctor after I moved, there was no way for me to get a refill on a lot of the medications I had been taking for a while. My body had an opportunity to detox from my medications over time. That detox was not a pretty process. I had already given up and giving up didn't work. So I dealt with the painful withdrawal period and detox from these medications.

Starting the year in a new place, surrounded by new people, and with a clear headspace was refreshing and exactly what I needed. The church had a tradition where they began each year with a 40 day Daniel's fast. I had no idea what a fast even was, so I really didn't know what I was doing or what I was getting myself into.

I was living with my sister and she was participating in the fast, so I of course had to follow along with the fast as well. I didn't have a source of income or any means to pay for my typical comfort foods or buy the soda I wanted. My only other option was to run back home to San Antonio and I was not going to do that nor was my spiritual mother going to let me give up! I realistically had no choice but to follow this Daniel's fast. What I didn't know was that this fast was a chance to truly experience a new desire for God's word while being spiritually healed.

I experienced more than I could have ever hoped for from my 40 day fast. In doing and learning the tradition, I began to physically understand the 'clarity' that my church congregation spoke about when doing this fast. I started finally hearing the Holy Spirit speaking to me. During these 40 days, I was dealing with my physical pain from the fibromyalgia and gout, and when you're fighting that type of pain, the pain that can't be fixed by medication alone, the only thing you can do is pray. That's when I was able to transition from a woman of faith to a prayer warrior.

The element of fasting is what shifted everything. At the first of the year, I had come off 22 medications, so I didn't have the side effects fogging up my thoughts in my mind to distract me. That was a major factor to this new found clarity. On top of that, all the meals in the Daniel's fast were strictly plant-based. Anything that grew from the ground was on the list of accepted foods; vegetables, water, all natural juices (yes they had to be pure with no added sugars - straight from the fruit!), no preservatives or chemicals in the food that I was consuming. There was no alcohol, or caffeine allowed either. That clean eating really amplified the clarity that I was experiencing.

After 40 days, I saw how much my life changed in just under a month. This fast and the habits I developed during the fast led me to a lot of breakthroughs in my life. I saw that I was actually able to do things and start **living**! It broke strongholds and generational curses that I had claimed for myself. It resulted in mental, physical and psychological healing from all that I suffered; depression, anxiety, psychosis, gout and fibromyalgia. I was given the clarity to understand that it would not be easy but it was possible. In addition, I had the strongest support system that helped me at my weakest moments. The enemy wants to isolate you and make you believe that you are alone in this world and no one cares about you, but the reality is you are never alone. God will send the right people into your life to help you get through your darkest moments. He will never leave or forsake you.

I craved more of that clarity, especially after I had been taking those pills for such a long time. I wanted more out of that lifestyle I had started to develop, so I ended up doing the 0 day fast total. My goal for the fast wasn't to lose weight, but I did end up losing about 80 pounds during those 40 days. But the biggest benefit I earned from that commitment to the fast was the mental and spiritual clarity. My confusion left, my thoughts weren't occupied by my feelings or the lies of the enemy.

I was consumed by the Word of God and the worship of God. I was physically being fed good food and spiritually I was being fed food for the soul. I actually began feeling like Frances, the Frances I was meant to be. Everything felt new and amazing, like a first breath in fresh air, or going from living in total darkness to opening one's eyes to the most picturesque garden.

I was 42 years old, having to follow my sister's rules and orders in her house, so there were times when I had little arguments with my sister and I felt like giving up this new lifestyle. But where would I have gone? I left my house, I left my vehicles, I left everything back in San Antonio. Financially I didn't have anything. I had to leave it to find my freedom, to find Frances. It wasn't an easy process, but I would do it again.

Having to leave my family here in San Antonio hurt like HELL. It was the hardest thing. I had raised two boys during the time I was with my partner. I was very present for my parents and for my aunt when she took over as the head of the family tree when my parents passed. I spent so much time with my godchildren to love them like my own. But if I had not left the family when I did, I would have been dead by now. I would have taken those pills - 22 pills a day. My liver would have been shocked and my kidneys shot. Weighing 80+ pounds more could have gotten to me too.

My spiritual parents and my family helped to keep me going in times where I was tempted or feeling defeated for one reason or the other. Being free from depression and anxiety was extremely life changing for me. I started breathing, walking and all in all living. Things that I stopped doing years ago. I was no longer taking shallow breaths and calling it life. I was able to take deep breaths and feel my lungs expand. I loved how I was feeling and I knew at that moment that I wanted to experience this clarity for the rest of life. The fast broke the chains that had caused doubt, pain, fear and sadness in my life.

During the 40 days I prayed, read His word and attended church. As much as possible I tried to stay with my church community so that I was never isolated and filled with self doubt that would deter me from completing that journey. I was surrounded by everything and everyone I needed to stay focused. I was given such clarity that I could hear a pin drop in the spirit.

During my fast I gave up anything that hindered my growth and healing. Usually I would watch television all day on the couch and watch life pass me by. When I moved in with my sister, I didn't have a television in the room so that decreased the temptation. Whenever I had the urge to go to the living room to watch television, I would go to church, read the bible, pray or listen to pastors on Youtube. Another bad habit was emotional eating of unhealthy foods.

In the past, I used food as a coping mechanism to deal with the negative emotions I was feeling. I was used to eating ice cream, soda and chips but for my fast I was allowed to only eat fruits and vegetables.

I was not supposed to have any sugars either so I mainly had water and unsweetened tea. Growing up when I misbehaved, which was often, my parents would punish me by taking away soda and sweetened tea and have me drink water only. So as an adult to have to drink water and unsweetened tea with every meal felt like a punishment. I was used to very greasy food and I did not like salads. There were a lot of times when I did not like what was at the table so I would eat the bare minimum. Each time I became stronger to resist the things that I at one point relied on. I knew exactly what I wanted and I was not giving up.

I turned to prayer when I felt hungry. I could feel and hear my stomach growling but I no longer felt the temptations that hunger brings when I prayed. It was so unreal. The louder my stomach growled, the more I got into the spirit. I used this as an incentive and encouragement in my most hungry moments. The hunger pains would test me and I started to learn and understand the authority that God has given us to ask and receive from Him. I felt as if I was being spiritually awakened when I prayed the pain away. I realized that God will give you exactly what you need if you have faith. It wasn't easy, but God got me through it. My prayers were being answered and I could see the good unfolding in my life because of my growing relationship with Him.

I was able to realize the authority we have not only in the spirit but in our body. My flesh had to submit to the fact that I was fasting and could no longer have or take part in certain things. I would tell myself the things I was not allowed to have or desire and equip myself with the word of God. I learned how to fill my soul rather than my stomach.

My family also helped to keep me occupied and distract my mind. My sister and brother in law helped me and welcomed me into their lives when I needed it the most. For the first time I was being taken care of instead of taking care of everyone else around me. I also gave up a lot of my friends as well, because they didn't understand the changes I was making to better myself. The couple friends that encouraged me through this time are still very dear friends of mine today. I had to come to a place of almost complete isolation to give me time to just focus on me and God.

My nieces loved to sing and praise God, so they would sing to me and just hearing their little voices was enough to keep me distracted and change my entire perspective. They were young and full of life. They kept me entertained, whether it was playing outside or hide and seek in the house. I would also help them with their homework and look after them.

Growing up, we didn't have any family vacations but that year we took our first family trip to Universal Studios. It meant so much to me. I felt so young and alive for the first time in my life. I had a community that loved and supported me. That was the point when I started to overcome all my negative emotions and learn who I was. I had to give up a lot to go on this journey to strengthen my relationship with God and find myself. I gave up a lot of my friends who were not supportive and lived the lifestyle that I was trying to turn away from. My true friends stuck by me and supported my decisions. It was necessary to fully isolate myself so that I could fully focus on me and God.

When I left San Antonio, I left behind a lot of painful memories, but I also left my oldest niece, cousin's and Godchildren who meant the world to me. They kept me going when I barely found the strength to leave my bed in the morning. It was hard, but I had to leave my security blanket in order to do the things that made me uncomfortable. I missed them so much but we would call on FaceTime often and that helped to keep me going during hard times. The normalcy of life had completely changed but it was necessary for my own self growth.

I gave up my home and everything I had, but in return I found myself and found my identity in Christ. Even after I completed the 40 days I continued the fast. I felt alive and had no desire to return to my old ways. It was like seeing a rose for the first time in my life and experiencing its beauty and color. I was afraid to put anything that was unhealthy and full of toxins in my body. I felt like I had 20/20 vision to see life and I did not want to do anything that would jeopardize that. I lost over 80 pounds and I started getting healthier and healthier. I was not taking pills anymore so my body felt truly cleansed from the 22 medications that I was taking and their negative effects. My body was rebuilding and I started to truly live without even realizing it.

CHAPTER 7
Looking for love

Working on myself from the fasting really gave me the opportunity to look at my life from a different perspective. From a young age I was convinced that I was born a certain way and only attracted to females. That belief was further instilled upon me as I grew up being bullied by boys I found attractive, and from being groomed at a young age by a lesbian. I didn't think it was ever a possibility for me to love or be loved by a man. I thought that there was no way ever in my mind that I would be with a man because my mind was predetermined that I had a specific lifestyle and preference when I never really explored that option.

José and I met at a gas station. At the time I was coming off all my medications. I don't even know how this man saw me, seriously. About a month after I had gotten to Dallas, I was looking like a hot mess. I was in the process where I had started losing some weight, but I was still probably around 350-360 lbs.

My sister had sent me to put gas in her vehicle. So I went to the nearest gas station dressed in a big baggy t-shirt and some shorts. When I went to put fuel in the tank, the gas cap had fallen out of my hand and rolled away on the ground. I had to hold down the trigger for the pump and thought 'Oh well, I'll go grab the gas cap when I finish putting gas in the tank'

This stranger walks up to me and hands me the gas cap, "Here. You dropped this." I looked up and we locked eyes and I was immediately hypnotized. I got lost in these beautiful green eyes. I was absolutely smitten. "I'm looking for a building near here, I'm an electrician. Do you know how to get there from here?" he asked me.

"I don't know where anything really is," I said. The gas station was at the corner just down the road from where my sister's house was, so I didn't know the area too well. "I just moved here about a month ago, so I really don't know where that's located" I explained.

"Oh, you just moved here?" Jose asked me. "Well, maybe I could show you around the city sometime."

I was just in a daze lost in his eyes. "Uh huh." He showed up out of nowhere and swept me off my feet. He gave me his number and I told him I would call him. I drove home right after and really sat down to think, "What is this? Am I serious? Do I really like him? Does he really want to take me out? I look like a mess!" I was completely torn. I had short choppy hair, flip flops and I was practically swimming in my shirt. Was he really flirting with me?

I really thought for a couple days before reaching out to him. I couldn't believe a handsome man had flirted with me. Was I really interested in him? I swore to God that I would never ever be loved by a man. But I sent him a simple, "Hello, this is Frances" text.

From there, he would call me and we'd talk on the phone. I felt like a teenager in love. Our first little date was at a Wingstop by where my sister lived. Of course I couldn't really tell her I was going out on dates. Well, they were lunch dates because I didn't have a vehicle, I was driving my sisters'.

I did end up getting married, but I also have to be transparent as far as how my marriage worked out. This man made lots of promises and to me he was such a handsome man. I think that's where I got hung up on him because he was so handsome and a handsome man said he loved me - that was something that I never thought to be possible.

He sure looked like my Prince Charming and so I felt for him deeply. In our relationship, we dated for possibly a week before I actually had sex with him and that was my first experience with being with a man. I told my sister that I met a guy and we had sex, and I knew something about it not being correct, but I thought to myself, "But, it was with a MAN."

I was really honest with Jose that I had only been with women and that, "I never thought I'd be interested in a man, but you're very interesting!" Jose was funny and he took the time to get to know what I liked. He knew how much I loved roses and he would buy me roses often to cheer me up. After I told my sister that I had sex with him, I had to cut him off. So our relationship didn't last too long. But he was funny and he was very adventurous and easy going. He liked being with me and doing whatever I enjoyed doing.

Jose and I would have lunch and talk on the phone and in the first few weeks of meeting this man, I had sex with him. I was kind of proud so I told my sister and that was one of the biggest mistakes of my life!

My sister was so livid that she contacted my spiritual parents, who were the pastors of our church. They drove an hour to me because we were in North Richland Hills and they lived south of Dallas and man I was in trouble! But it was almost like I had reached a goal to prove my past experiences to be wrong. I almost asked them, "Aren't you proud?"

To me it felt like I conquered having that experience, but when my spiritual parents came, I learned really quickly that I wasn't supposed to do that. But I think I wanted to prove to my old self wrong that I wouldn't ever be loved by a man or have sex with a man, I thought it was impossible. So I wanted to experience that.

My pastors, especially my spiritual Mama, she lectured me, "You're fasting and you're trying to get right with God. That is not correct. You're supposed to wait until you're married!" Lord Jesus, I heard it all! My spiritual father was so upset. He wanted to know how the enemy had trapped me to have done that. Like, have you ever seen green piercing eyes on a smooth-talking, light complexion, southern man? C'mon. That's how!

Jose offered to let me move in with him so we could continue to see each other. "Go pack whatever clothes you have, and I'll pick you up," he said to me. He knew all there was to know about me and my past and he was very caring and loving. But I explained to him that I was trying to get right with God and I wasn't supposed to be having sex before marriage. Now I feel like Jose's offer to run away together was a temptation. I believe the enemy was trying to take me out of the will of God, because had I run off with Jose, I wouldn't be where I am now in my spiritual journey. God only knows where I would have been.

I had lost focus on building my personal relationship with God. At the time I was fasting and focusing on controlling the flesh. I had to learn how to turn the flesh off and stand completely on the Word of God. I had to learn how to separate emotions, which are part of the flesh to what the Bible says. For once, I wanted to live entirely in the Will of God.

When I met Jose, I was only 20 days into this new Daniels fast. We both enjoyed each other's personalities. He enjoyed that I was a little outgoing and he liked my personality. He was more introverted and would often tell me, "Frances, I would love to be the way you are. You inspire me to want to be like you."

I felt ashamed because I was really trying to get right with God, but as humans we fall and we fail. My spiritual parents and my sister pretty much forbid me to see him. I couldn't contact him, I had him blocked on Facebook, he would show up and I couldn't go outside to see him. Again, I was living with my sister and she was ready to tattle on me like I was a teenager.

Imagine someone that had been so independent, raised and supported a family while caretaking for their parents all while working full time transition to now sharing a bedroom with their youngest niece - talk about a humbling experience! I had rules to follow as a 40 year old. It was really difficult.

Eventually I met someone new. Early one Sunday morning I got a Facebook friend request from some gentleman and I noticed he had a few mutual friends from church with me, so I accepted his request. Due to my ex, I had deleted my old Facebook and this was a new account with new positive people in my life and church friends. This guy showed up to church a few hours later. I told my sister, "Remember how I got a friend request this morning? He's here!" and my sister replied, "Oh my goodness, maybe that will be your husband!'"

He was about 10 years younger than me. During the service, he and I made contact quite a bit and sure enough he reached out to me on messenger and he eventually asked me out. I thought to myself, 'I guess this is a man that God wants in my life.' He attends church regularly, he's active in worship and he plays piano for the praise band."

We would text and call each other on messenger and sometimes he'd call me while he was playing beautiful worship songs on the keyboard and singing. We would go out to dinner some nights too. My spiritual mother wasn't too content with our relationship, but he was very respectful and a perfect gentleman. Him being 10 years younger, he did show some insecurities.

I would often take the $12 megabus to visit my family in San Antonio. When I traveled, that's when a lot of his insecurities would surface. "Are you sure you're not going to go see your ex-girlfriend?" He would ask me. Of course I was so over that. I would usually stay for a long weekend or a week with my family and I would stay in communication with my boyfriend every step of the way.

"I'm leaving San Antonio, I'm back on the bus. I should be back to Dallas in 4-5 hours," I would text to him.

As soon as I would tell him I was en route back to my sister's house, he would head to my sister's house and show up and wait for me. He was so anxious. My sister would call me not even an hour into my ride back home, "He is already here waiting outside the house for you." He really adored me, but sometimes his insecurities were a bit overbearing.

I wouldn't have been surprised if this man kissed the ground I walked on, he was very adorable and truly cared for me. He asked me to marry him and of course I said yes. I had met him at church, he was a Godly man and I truly believed he was who God had handpicked for me to be married to. He worked really hard to make our wedding happen. He even bought me a dress and a ring. We had a date picked out and everything.

He loved me, but I wasn't really sure if I had loved him as much as he had loved me. There was also our age difference that played a factor in our daily communication and priorities. Back then I even looked older than I do now just because of my lifestyle choices at that time and all the stress I had recently been through. Visually, he kind of looked like he could have been my son! In my heart I didn't feel like it was 100% a fit, but I also wanted to please God.

He felt like the person that God had sent for me. He loved and was faithful with God. We had go to our pastor, my spiritual father and went through marriage counseling. Before we actually got married we answered all the questions, "Do you find her attractive? Do you really love her?" He answered yes to the above. But when I was asked, I said, "I find him a little attractive, but I love him." I was being honest, but he was totally opposite from what I am now attracted to. My spiritual father emphasized that if our marriage was going to work out, "if you want to marry him, you have to really be attracted to him. There has to be an attraction." Granted, there was some attraction, but I honestly believed he was who God sent for me. I wanted to abide by God's wishes and do everything correctly this time.

About a month before the wedding, I got a text from an unknown number, "Hello, Frances." I of course texted back asking who this mystery person was that had my number. "It's José" they replied. My heart sank. I guess he had gotten a new phone, but he saved my number. He couldn't message me from his original number because I had him blocked. He asked me how I was doing, and I was trying to be strong and off-putting. José would make me weak in the knees.

"Don't contact me. I'm getting married in a month!" I replied to him. I was a little dramatic, but I wasn't trying to sabotage God's plan for me to marry my fiancé. Then I dreaded answering the phone when I saw that he was now calling me.

"Please don't. I love you," he said.

Those darn words. I can still recall how he said them. They just stuck with me. "I gotta go," I said as I hung up on him. I blocked his new number almost immediately as my fiancé walked towards me seeing the look of shock on my face.

He and I were so excited about the wedding just being weeks away before I got José's call. Poor guy came up to me after I hung up the phone to ask what was wrong. I was stressed! How was I supposed to act with an emotional blow like this all of a sudden?

"What's wrong? Did I do something wrong to you?" He asked.

"I replied, "No, you didn't do anything wrong to me. I'm just tired." I had played it off so I could continue about my night. But José's words were still echoing like a broken record in my mind. He said them so sincerely, too.

My fiancé and I continued our routine of going to church together and continuing our dates and finishing wedding plans. About a month before our wedding date, I finally figured out how I felt. I just didn't love him as much as I wanted to. " I don't want to marry you" I told him. He wasn't a bad looking guy, he was lovely and kind, but he wasn't José.

The Holy Spirit was really starting to talk to me more at this time. I had thought about my feelings for them both and I was actively fasting and praying over this decision. When I fast, I'm able to hear the Holy Spirit more clearly. IN my mind, I was no longer confused, I knew I didn't love My fiancé like I did José and that it wasn't fair to him or myself to put us through that. I was just trying to play the role of the good christian and I felt like I would be settling with him. Through my fasting and prayer, I was able to determine that marriage wasn't really what I wanted for my life.

For the next few days, He would drive up to the house wanting to talk to me. My sister felt bad for him and would try to get me to talk to him, "Frances, He is at the house again." I had nothing more to tell him besides that I didn't really love him with my whole heart.

Shortly after I called off the wedding, that's when I moved back to San Antonio. It was in October when I finally got settled in back in San Antonio with my job and my church family. I was working full time and attending church as usual.

CHAPTER 8
Finding God's grace

In 2015, when I made the decision to move back to San Antonio. I was unemployed at the time with only $26 to my name. A friend gave me a ride to the city, and in exchange for driving me, I gave them $25 - leaving me with only $1. I moved in with my cousin near the same neighborhood where I grew up. I borrowed her daughter's high school vehicle after we got it working again! to go job searching.

I was able to find a job at a shelter for teenagers where I played the role of a house mother. I felt a sense of purpose was being fulfilled by caring for these teenage girls who had been through so much in life. Shortly after I started working this new job, I found a church home in the community as well.

I was attending church regularly and enjoying the work at the shelter. It was at that point that I finally reconnected with what my purpose was and what it felt like to be valued. I had been a provider for most of my life, but I reached a whole new level of independence. This was the first time in my life that I was doing things for just myself. Neither my family nor my friends were dependent upon me. I didn't have to support anyone else. Everything I did day in and day out was for Frances.

On my first visit to the church, I distinctly heard the Holy Spirit say to me, "Walk the church grounds and pray." So, I walked the church grounds and prayed to obey God. As a woman of God, I know that he does reward obedience. The teenage shelter was a few minutes down the road from the church I attended, so I began walking the grounds every single day before work.

I would arrive at the church around noon, and walk until 1:30 pm right before going to work at 2 pm. For many years, I did that every day except on Sundays. Whether it was hot, cold, or raining - I did as the Holy Spirit commanded. At the time, I wasn't in the best of health. As a result of a damaged meniscus in my right knee, I had to drag my right leg while walking because I could not bend my knee enough to walk.

Despite the pain from all the walking, I still prayed and I still followed God's instructions. Within months, I was given keys to the church house from the pastors to go inside the church to pray as well. I was so amazed and in awe when they gave me that access because I did not own a home, but yet, I had the key to the church. That was a learning experience for me to stay obedient when God gives directions. I didn't need material things, but there was something greatly symbolic about being handed a key to God's house, especially when I didn't even have a key to my own home yet. Having a key to God's house but not owning a house was an incredible privilege that God granted me.

The church congregation immediately accepted me as family when I joined the church. A sister from church who was going to buy a new car passed her used vehicle to me, so I could continue to make the payments but also have a newer vehicle. This church was like a huge family that welcomed me, loved me, and helped me. These were the blessings that came along with my obedience to God hearing the Holy Spirit telling me to pray at the church grounds. This church is still my home church to this day. I have become a prayer warrior since then and an intercessor.

On Christmas Day of 2016, I received a few obligatory "Merry Christmas" text messages from family and friends. While I was replying to every message, sending my own holiday wishes to everyone, I came across an unfamiliar number again. Upon asking who this number belonged to - Deja vú! It was José again.

"Are you married?" he wrote.

Of course I responded, "No." He wasted no time in dialing my number to talk to me.

"Well, what happened?" José asked.

"I couldn't stop thinking about you," I explained.

I could tell that got him excited, "Well, can we meet for lunch?" I was open to meeting him for lunch, but he still lived in Dallas.

"We can meet for lunch, but you're gonna have to drive to San Antonio because that's where I live now" and to my surprise, he said he'd drive up to meet me.

As the days passed, I became so anxious but more so excited for our lunch date. "Oh my God, he really does love me. I cannot wait to see him" I thought. Our lunch date was in early January, almost two years after we had first met. He confessed that he loved me this whole time, but with my spiritual journey I had to cut him off and that broke his heart. We talked for hours and eventually talked about my engagement to the other guy.

"Will you marry me now?" he asked me.

"José, are you serious?!" I rebutted. The last time we saw each other, he was asking me to run away and move in with him, but marriage was a much bigger commitment. But he knew the marriage commitment was what I truly wanted as a Christian.

"Maybe we can," I told him. "But we'll have to talk through some things and see where this goes."

January had passed and we were still taking turns traveling to see each other between San Antonio and Dallas for weeks enjoying our rekindled relationship. In February, he formally proposed to me and made it official. I had already told him that I would marry him, because he had waited all this time for me, and he was showing up and he chased me. He did want this relationship.

We got married a month later on March 25th. We had a beautiful church wedding and reception. He was living in the Dallas/Fort Worth area at the time while I was in San Antonio. He promised me the world. He worked as a contracted electrician so he had one or two contracts that he had to finish before he could move to San Antonio. Together we looked at future homes for us once he was able to move and we talked about where we wanted to live.

Every weekend after we got married, he would drive up to San Antonio to be with me. After a few months, his contract jobs had more complications and he was working longer and more difficult hours. That made the 4 hour drive to San Antonio a difficult drive. Every weekend turned into every other weekend visits after the honeymoon phase wore off. Eventually, our scheduled visit times just faded away.

Recently, I was able to see him and we talked through a lot of our issues. Of course he and I both wanted this marriage to work. He expressed how often and deeply he was praying for our marriage. But we were living almost two completely separate lives. The logistics of joining our households after our wedding ceremony just hadn't come together and time had caused us to drift apart from one another.

I didn't want to think about divorce as an option just yet, because I was afraid that the church, not so much God, but rather the church would again reject me. My church family in San Antonio and my family had all known about my marriage with José. My church family had gotten to see him here and there. He even volunteered to do the rewiring of all the electricity for the church building. My family has been able to call on him for electrical questions and he has been more than willing to help them. He had a good heart, he was a faithful man and I loved him so dearly.

My pride got the better of me at that point. I thought if he loved me, then he would come and show up! If he loves me, he'll call. If he loves me, he'll text. Despite my doubts, I clung to the idea that this type of relationship would work. Even if he shows up once a month, we're still married, right?

Because of who I was in the church, I was trying to cover it up even more. I was this prayer warrior, an intercessor who had a reserved seat in the front row. My reputation was on the line, and I wanted to look like I had everything under control. So I went along with it. Of course, people would ask, "Frances, how's your husband?" I would reply, "He's doing great, just busy." Sometimes what I really wanted to say was, "Well, when *YOU* hear from him, you tell me how he's doing!"

I also had my work to deal with. So if he didn't call, text, or anything like that, I would just go back to keeping myself occupied with my seemingly separate life. Since I was afraid he would not respond to my calls or messages, I usually just left him alone. I had an overwhelming fear that I might get hurt again if I reached out to him. My internal dialogue was my defense mechanism; "If he wants to call, he'll call… if he wants to text, he'll text…" After a while that dialogue started to tell me, "if he wants to show up, he'll show up." I didn't go out searching for him because again; I didn't want to set myself up for failure.

I was really struggling with the situation of filing for a divorce. I wanted to serve God, but I did not want to disappoint him by ending my marriage although it just wasn't working out. The day finally came where I broke the news to José that I wanted to be divorced. I didn't want anything from the divorce, I just wanted to be done with the debate of when our union was truly going to start.

It was during that time when I met Pastor Kim. I had come across one of her sermons where she brought up divorce. She doesn't encourage divorce, but she encourages that regardless if we failed in our marriage, God can still use us. At that point in our marriage, José had practically ghosted me. He wouldn't even text me or initiate a call with me. I wouldn't know about his day or what he was doing. In my marriage, I was beginning to feel abandoned and rejected.

At church, many people looked up to me as the prayer warrior that I am, but I had all these complications going on internally because I had learned many times in my life that I will not mix emotions with the Word of God. When the Holy Spirit speaks to me, he speaks to me very clearly, but it's not an emotion or a feeling. It's a very clear drive and voice, there is no confusion, mixed feelings or sense of doubt. The Holy Spirit is not a feeling. At that point, I had to remind myself that I serve a mighty God and that he does not fail. We fail, but God does not.

I had to come to terms with the fact that just because we fell short in our marriage, that was not going to stop who God created me to be. For most of my life, I struggled with my identity. Now, I believe that one of my strongest things in serving Christ and praying for people is that now I know my identity in Christ. In knowing my identity, no demon, no hell, no witch, no warlock or stronghold can take that identity away from who Christ has made me to be.

Emotions have to be put to the side when you're working spiritually. The enemy comes to kill, steal and destroy and when he does that, he starts at the mind. Whatever the mind thinks, the rest of your body follows. The mind controls the heart. and the heart controls the emotions. I've learned that yes, there has to be a balance. I'm not a cold person, per se, but I also have to recognize those shifts in my life so clearly that I can say to myself, "Wait, this is an emotion, it's not what God is saying to me."

I have to really refocus. I know that when I fast, the Holy Spirit speaks so much clearer to me. He doesn't ever *stop* speaking. But when you're not focused and you are preoccupied with life and your emotions based on your surroundings, it's so easy to block out what the Holy Spirit is communicating to you.

As an intercessor, as a prayer warrior, this is the main reason why I fast so that I can have that clear direction and clearer mind. When I fast, I don't put in all those toxic chemicals into my body that comes with processed foods. A year later, french fries from a fast food restaurant look the same as they do when they're handed to you in the drive thru lane when they were freshly made. All the chemicals and toxins that we're putting in our bodies also cloud our signal with the Holy Spirit. I do love my ice cream and my soda, but I have periods of intentional fasting from those types of foods that don't feed the soul.

In fasting, I believe that God has elevated me even higher than I could imagine. There is such a thing as the "Spiritual Realm" and hearing the Word of God. God does speak to everyone, but are we making ourselves available and preparing ourselves to actually hear?

Personally, I believe when you feed yourself all these toxins and chemicals; sugar, soda, convenience foods, artificial this and that - it has to make your mind foggy. It can really cloud your mind. I try my best to stick to the Daniel's fast when I fast. Without sugar in my diet, I have felt elevated to a higher spiritual realm in my prayer work.

I don't believe that God has anyone specifically planned out for me, but I'm believing that God is moving me in a whole different direction. I have always wanted to be able to please God. I've spoken to my current spiritual mother, and she advised me to give my marriage a true try "so that you will never ever have to wonder if you are correct. Spend time with him, just the two of you. Put your phone down and have no distractions. Don't worry about anything but you two." We tried, and that was a wonderful weekend, and the next week was good. But by the second week, going into Wednesday and Thursday, that's when it felt like he forgot that I existed again.

CHAPTER 9
The redemption

On my social media, I post videos to encourage people from all over the world in their faith and personal journeys. I don't get all dolled up and rehearse, I speak from what God has put in my heart to give for the day.

In 2019, I heard a testimony shared by a Pastor about how she is still serving God despite being divorced. Some people were not accepting of her testimony but some were. Her words woke me up, and made me realize that even though I had failed in my marriage, I could still serve God. So I felt like I had been released from shame and embarrassment which was holding me back. I was able to continue to grow deeper and deeper into this prayer warrior and be who I am today.

Thanks to God, I now have the privilege of praying for thousands of people over social media. It is God and one act of obedience that brought me to this point. One act of obedience led me being trusted with bigger things. This is why obedience is so important. In between, yes, we fail and we fall short of the glory, but no one is perfect. As hard as we try not to fall, we do. Nevertheless, obeying God is rewarded.

Regardless of my failures and my bad decisions, I have gained my identity as a result of walking into my purpose and knowing who I am.

I have a routine that I follow: whenever a name comes to me, I pray. It has even come to the point where I wake up at 4 am to pray and intercede for my pastors, my loved ones, my family, my friends, my church, the ministry, and whoever God lays on my heart. Moreover, I also pray for individuals who are currently asking for prayer on social media pages, as well as all the private messages that I receive on a daily basis.

I carry a heavy anointing where I can walk into the room and people are delivered. It is the Holy Spirit within me. I've learned how to fast and how to pray. I can do an absolute fast for three days without water. I am now able to see visions and pray for others. Once, a friend of mine was having some problems. Thus, her friend reached out to me and asked me to pray for our friend. At the moment I didn't know why I responded this way, but I responded by saying, "Okay, I'm going in."

I don't waste time texting back or responding to people who call in with urgent prayers. As I've experienced in my own life, many situations that require prayer are time sensitive. As I closed my eyes and prayed, I was able to visualize what my friend was actually experiencing. With my eyes closed, I begin to intercede and pray, covering her with the blood of Jesus. I was able to see her in this vehicle, and I saw it swaying side to side on the highway. I remember pulling the door open and grabbing her by the arm, to pull her out. I saw what looked like bright yellow lights on the road.

About two months later, I spoke with both of them and she told me what had happened that night. She explained that she was a passenger when the driver was driving recklessly. She was wanting out of the vehicle but was unable to open her car door. She pushed, kicked and tried to open the car door, but couldn't, and then suddenly, this force came out of nowhere and opened the door. While opening the car door, the door handle broke. Then I was like, oh Lord Jesus, I remember opening the car door in the Spirit. She was able to escape through the opened door. So then I was like, "Oh my God, are you serious? She says she has the door handle to prove that it was me who broke the handle. I said "No, I didn't break it."

The anointing I carry was revealed to me once again, so I believe God confirmed that part of me. I believe He wanted me to know that I do carry a heavier anointing.

I don't see it, but people tell me. I am very humble. I will never and you will never hear me boast. Often people would ask for prayer, and I would close my eyes and it's almost like I'm walking into the situation or where they are. As it turned out, I really was unaware that that was what was really going on. This woke me up, it let me know that what I'm seeing is real when I'm praying. So it was a confirmation of what I had been praying and seeing in the Spirit.

Now, when people contact me or when God shows me someone, I hear names of people and I pray for those things. Sometimes the Holy Spirit wakes me up, and I will see somebody's face and immediately begin to pray for them. Once I tell him/her about how the Holy Spirit inspired me to pray for you, in the middle of the morning, they will confirm that something really did happen at that time.

"For the time will come when you will say,
'Blessed are the childless women, the wombs that never bore
and the breasts that never nursed!"
- Luke 23:29

Because of my lifestyle when I was young, I knew I was never going be able to bear a child. A lot of my personal pain throughout those relationships had stemmed from my desire to want children of my own. Deep down inside I longed to have children.

I physically never felt the kicks of carrying a child. I've never felt the actual birthing pains. Because of my personal faith journey, I have a lot of spiritual children. In the spirit, I have felt those pains. I have walked with people through their midnight hour and I have been with them in their anguish and pain that they're going through in their lives, just as a mother would. A lot of people do have biological mothers, but many mothers have abandoned their children, or they haven't become the mother that they need. In the spiritual realm, I have mothered so many.

I believe that will give someone hope. I feel the enemy stole the opportunity to be a biological mother from me because of my sinful ways of living in a same sex relationship. The opportunity to physically bring a life into this world and birth a child was stolen from me.

After hearing this woman's explanation of Luke 23:29, I had an 'Ah-Ha' moment. The devil never took that opportunity from me. I have so many children now, whether I felt those kicks or I actually felt the pain of giving birth. I have still felt like that mother. God still gave me that opportunity to be the mom I always wanted to be.

My work as an intercessor started from the day I realized just how important my mother's prayers were. I no longer have my mother but when I pray, I pray like a mother for her children. When someone comes to me or if I'm praying for someone on my prayer list, it's not a nonchalant, "Yes, God. Help them in their ways." I pray for their core, their soul, their mind, and body. Some days I don't even pray for myself as much as intensely as I do for other people. This may sound silly, but whatever prayer petition I receive, I pray, but I pray with ***everything in me!***

I activate angels when I pray because I know I have their protection. Even for the smallest or most distant matters from me, I pray with the same intensity that causes miracles, because I know how important the prayers of a mother are. I get prayer requests from all sorts of people covering all sorts of requests. Whether it's a family member recovering from a life-threatening situation or someone requesting that I pray for the life of a rat stuck in a glue trap that they passed by. No prayer request is insignificant and no prayer request is less.

If anyone hands me a prayer request, no matter how big, small, or silly, you better believe I'm going to pray for it, and I'm going to put my all into it! I make myself available to listen and pray. It could be 5pm here, but it's someone's midnight hour somewhere; and I will walk you through it!

Being an intercessor is not the title of who you are and it's not about how perfect your faith journey may look to others or wanting to make an impression, it's about being available for God's children when they need you. God knows you. He knows your heart. To me, that's what an intercessor is, and it's all for the honor and Glory of God and what He can do.

God parted the Red Sea to that they could walk through it You need to believe that God will make a way, because he will. For when we think something is ending, it is usually the beginning of something greater that God has in store for us.

I'm at a transitory time in my life where I can feel a build up from God. I'm standing, and I'm waiting and trusting God in this process, because I know that he is taking me somewhere greater. I thoroughly believe that God is preparing me for my calling. We serve a mighty God that will not fail.

If you would like to submit a prayer request to Frances,
please know that no concern is too big, too silly, or too small.

Please send a written request to
helllostanother1@gmail.com

NOTES/JOURNAL
CONCLUSION

The enemy comes to kill, steal and destroy. We have people that are so lost and don't even know who they are and they're going through the motions of life, contemplating their purpose but deep down inside they know who they are truly meant to be. Maybe they're afraid to fail and they may not be consistent but they're getting toward who they really want to be.

No matter where you're at in life, if you're just beginning your faith journey, if you're revisiting Christ, or if this is all new to you, just know that you're welcome to reach out to me to pray for you. This is a safe space for you for whatever you need it to be, whether you're taking notes, learning how you pray, or working on discovering your identity in Christ.

This is a safe space. You are loved. You can heal. Once you know your identity in Christ, no hell, no demon, and nobody can take that away from you.